Your Essential Handbook for Exploring New Zealand

Mohamedy R. Ahmed

In the desert of doubt, find oases of hope and perseverance.

Stay updated with literary awards globally; they highlight quality literature from various cultures and languages.

Practice patience; good things often take time.

Stay consistent in branding; it ensures recognizability and trust.

Introduction

This book is a comprehensive resource for travelers looking to explore the hidden gems and unique experiences of the North Island of New Zealand. The guide offers insider tips, self-drive suggestions, and valuable insights to help travelers make the most of their journey. The guide emphasizes the importance of self-drive, timing, preparation, and local knowledge for a successful travel experience. It provides practical travel tips, including advice on avoiding hypothermia at the beach, saving money and back while traveling, and ensuring beach access for all visitors. Additionally, the guide introduces an additional travel idea to enhance the experience even further.

Throughout the guide, specific destinations and activities are highlighted. Readers are encouraged to explore Auckland beyond its city limits, with mentions of tramping, kayaking at night, and attractions like Takapuna Beach, The Hillary Track, kayaking to Rangatoto, and Shakespear Park. Russell's significance as New Zealand's starting point and its scenic beauty are emphasized. The Coromandel Peninsula offers scenic drives and specific attractions like Whangamata, Treasure Island, Whiritoa, Onemana, and Opoutere.

The Waitomo section details an adventure in the Waitomo Caves, including the famous Waitomo Caves themselves and the option of black water tubing. Rotorua invites travelers to explore mud pools and engage in mountain biking adventures at the Rotorua mountain bike center. The Tongariro Crossing is showcased as a renowned hike not to be missed. The Whanganui section focuses on the Whanganui River and suggests kayak or canoe trips for a deeper connection with the land.

New Plymouth is introduced as a destination with unique accommodation, rugged coastline, skiing, and surfing opportunities. Martinborough invites readers to indulge in wine, cheese, and stunning views, along with attractions like the Putangirua Pinnacles and Castlepoint Beach & Lighthouse. Wellington, the capital city, offers cultural experiences, beer tours, and a visit to the Weta Workshop.

Practical information includes a map of the North Island with hyperlinked Google Maps, New Zealand public holidays, and additional resources for travelers. The guide presents a comprehensive itinerary, insider tips, and valuable insights for travelers seeking to uncover the North Island's hidden treasures and unique experiences.

Contents

Unique Kiwi tips and experiences you can get at any time.

Perhaps the most common question I get from those wanting to consider a trip to NZ is, "How does NZ compare to other countries in the world – I hear it's a lot like …."

Simply put, the answer to this question, is akin to squashing up Canada, America and Australia, combining all their unique attributes (Mountains, beaches and ruggedness), and placing them in a land mass that takes 3-5 hours to drive across, and 2-3 days to drive the length of. In other words, spectacular and easy to get a great experience from.

When going to NZ there are many good ideas of things to try aside from the looking at the awesome scenery. Below are some additional suggestions that will add to your experience of New Zealand that cannot be found anywhere else in the world.

Self drive

On a trip to NZ no matter what your age, do the self-drive option. A very important point is to remember that NZ'ers drive on the opposite side of the road to North America. This means you will be driving on the left hand side of the road. This is okay on major highways which have a center line to remind you (along with cars coming the other way), but NZ has many areas that are not marked by a center line, and are remote, so make sure you are well rested before getting behind the wheel.

Just like other countries, New Zealand police love to catch speeders. Especially by hiding their cars behind flax bushes on the side of the road. If you want to avoid a friendly chat along with a donation to the New Zealand Police force, mind your speed (it is only 100km an hour as maximum speed in NZ).

The other thing to keep in mind, is that although NZ looks like an insignificant blip on the world map, the roads are narrow with lots of corners. This means trips that are an hour in duration, can often feel like 3. Therefore, leave lots of time and don't try to make an itinerary that results in feeling rushed. Reading in the car for this reason is also ill advised (literally), unless being car sick is a thing you enjoy.

Tour companies in NZ are really great, but you are stuck on their schedule and their travel directions. New Zealand is best suited to flying by the seat of your pants and driving. Many of the best experiences my friends and I had growing up in this land were simply found by driving and stopping at will. It is after all, possible to drive the entire length of NZ in 3 days (you'll be a bit tired if you do, but still, it's possible).

Don't be put off by my words of caution above. If you are from another country, New Zealand's roads are not that busy and the drivers fairly courteous (as long as you are not on a passing lane - you'll see what I mean when you get there).

Time is of the essence

Book more time to spend in NZ than you think you'll need. The amount of friends who decided to travel to New Zealand and wistfully realize they should have allocated more time, is unbelievable. Sure, New Zealand on a map may look like a small blip, insignificant and cute in comparison to the continents of the world, but don't be fooled. It takes a long time to drive to places due to the windey roads and once you arrive, the places can really encourage you to stay. If you are trying to see everything in this book then you will surely feel rushed and wish you had more time. As a guide, three weeks is probably the bare minimum to get the most out of just the North Island!

Timing is everything

The best chance at good weather is the end of February early March. The summer officially starts in December but with the Maori name for New Zealand being Aotearoa (which translates to "the land of the long white cloud"), one can expect a lot of rain at certain times of the year. If you have a choice, choose February or March. Good quality rain gear is essential no matter when you choose to travel. You have been warned.

Preparation makes the difference

Pack for all seasons. Even in summer, New Zealand has a number of different climates and on any given day can have many different weather systems come through. You won't need your snow gear in summer, but what feels like a cool Fall/Autumn day can be expected at least a few times during what should be summer temperatures. For those of you who remember the band *Crowded House*, "Four Seasons in one day" is an apt reflection of the climate one can experience here.

Flags at the beach

Beaches can be dangerous. The safest place to swim is between the flags (they are red and yellow and easy to see on a beach). If you are at a beach with waves, the least safe place to swim is where it's calm (counterintuitive I know). Calm water at a beach with surf at it, indicates a hole and is where water is moving out to sea. If for whatever reason you are finding it difficult to return to shore, raise your hand above your head and do not keep swimming. Someone will rescue you.

Every year tourists drown on NZ and Australian beaches, to avoid being a statistic, be sure to know how to swim if going in the ocean and always swim between the flags where ever possible.

Unique tastes

Food and Drink:

If you are going to NZ, there are several things one must try.

1. A steak and cheese pie (or mince and cheese) from any of the many bakeries in NZ. The best ones have the pastry look a pale color. Avoid bakeries selling yellow pastry pies.
2. Jet planes. These are a great candy and unique to NZ. Try them if you have a sugar craving, you won't be disappointed. (they are in the supermarket under the brand name PASCAL and before you ask, this is not a paid advertisement).
3. L&P - short for Lemon and Paeroa. This pop (drink) tastes like a lemonade ice block. Delicious and only available in NZ. Find it at any corner store, gas station or supermarket. This is non-alcoholic and also available at gas stations and supermarkets (it was invented in the town of Paeroa which you will pass through if travelling between Whangamata and Hamilton). Another fantastic alternative is Ginger beer (also non-alcoholic). Bundaberg makes the best version of this.
4. Ice Cream: If you want to truly experience a kiwi summer, then one must eat tip top (the brand) hokey pokey ice cream. Trust me, you won't be disappointed.
5. Beer: New Zealand is known for its wines, but its beers are also amazing. From the many craft breweries one can find a taste that will hit the spot, and if you want something more akin to mainstream ale/lager, then try speights, db export gold, or steinlager pure. Best of all, NZ sells beer and wine in their supermarkets so when you go shopping you won't need to take extra trips to get the supplies.
6. Cheese: Not being made from milk powder, the real milk taste ensures the cheaper cheeses still taste amazing.

Edam and Colby are two varieties that do well on sandwiches and if you are after something with a bit more bite to it, then Tasty is your go to. If you are after the more extravagant versions, there are plenty of options all available at supermarkets.

7. Lamb: Easy to buy at the supermarkets, this is a 'must get" whilst travelling through NZ. With the human population outnumbered by sheep (there are approximately 16 million sheep and only 4 million humans), finding a good cut of lamb is as simple as going to the supermarket and picking some up.

8. Whitebait fritters: Yes, there is such a thing and this is truly unique to NZ. When driving you will see signs up on the side of the road advertising this NZ delicacy (mostly in the southern/ central half of the North Island). Whitebait are small little fish about the size of half a babies pinky, and are unique to NZ. You said you wanted the inside tip, so there it is.

9. Feijoas: This fruit is only in season for a short period of time. If you see them for sale, then buy some. Do not eat the outside (it doesn't taste very good). Instead slice them in half and eat the centers. There are also non-alcoholic and alcoholic drinks made from this fruit and these are available in stores throughout the year.

10. Roadside stalls: These are a great place to get anything from avocados to fruit. There are often "honesty boxes", which means you simply leave the money at the stand for the things you buy. Since you will be driving, you are going to see a lot of these scattered throughout the country and it is a very cost effective way to secure awesome produce.

Knowledge is the power

At every town and city in NZ there is an information building, manned (or "womaned") by some knowledgeable locals. Whilst I have covered a number of ideas for unique things to do, if you are in a place that is not mentioned in this book, simply visit the local information building and let the great volunteers assist you in finding something to your liking.

Save your back

When you arrive in New Zealand there are several great duty free shops before you clear customs. These are just as well priced as the options you will find at the country you departed from.

Save yourself the hassle of lugging bottles of booze unnecessarily on the plane and looking like a party animal. Instead purchase them just before you exit. As an added bonus, they often have deals where you get freebees if you buy enough. NZ's duty limits for alcohol are 4.5 litres of wine or beer, and. 3 x 1.125 litre bottles of spirits. Given the tax you will have to pay once in NZ on such items, my advice is to stock up.

Save your money

Tipping is not part of the culture, so when you see the price and think "that's a bit pricey", it has the tip included. Do your pocket book and New Zealand's culture a favor and only tip if you really, really, really, think the service made you feel like a King or Queen. If you are pleased or happy with the service it is always gratefully accepted.

What the "Wh"

Anything that starts with "Wh" in a place name is pronounced as an "F". That includes Whakapapa. For the sake of keeping this G rated I will leave the pronunciation of that word for your own experimentation. I provide this information for you simply so you will seem less like a tourist and more like a travel aficionado.

Hypothermia avoidance

NZ is perceived to be warmer than it is. In short, unless you like to shrivel up like a dried prune, bring a wetsuit! The water is cold. This is not Hawaii and even in the middle of summer, the water is best referred to as "refreshing".

Beach access is for all!

Due to New Zealand's long coast line, a rule was created by Queen Victoria, called the "Queens chain" (you will notice a theme in NZ about the Queen). It allows for public access to 99% of New Zealand's beaches, which means there are very few private beaches.

The rule states that 20 meters above the high tide mark is to be reserved for the public to enjoy along all of New Zealand's coast line (apparently a length of chain was 20 meters in those days). Now of course, a lot of the beaches are inaccessible without crossing someone's land, but if you can make it there without doing that, the beach is there for you to enjoy!

In every beach side community you will find white marker posts indicating public access to the beach. That way when you are travelling and want to see the water and put your feet on the sand, just drive towards the water where you will quickly find a way to access it.

ADDITIONAL TRAVEL IDEA TO REALLY STEP IT UP

This books focus is on the North Island of NZ, but if you are travelling from the Northern Hemisphere, then this additional stop can be the most amazing way to take your trip to another level. What is this amazing stop? Tahiti. Set on the equator, this area of many islands is on the way to New Zealand (provided you live up

North), and is one of the most spectacular places I have had the pleasure of travelling to. With golden sands, crystal clear water and amazingly friendly people, this is tourism at its best. I will leave for you to further research, but I will say, it is one of the few places that I would love to visit again.

Now that we have the insider tips to making your NZ trip a fun time, let me get to the real reason you bought this book. Where to go and what to see….

Auckland - It's more than just a city.

Tramp like a mad man and kayak at night, game on.

Pronounced: Ork land

Why you should go: Nightlife, great views, great food, on the way to where you need to go

History/ Meaning:

New Zealand seems to have had an issue with deciding on its capital, with Russell, then Auckland and finally Wellington (in 1865) all having the prestigious honor.

Auckland became the capital of New Zealand after the initial town of Russell was deemed not to be a good fit in 1841 after the signing of the Waitangi treaty (the agreement between the native Maori and the white man over how land was going to be sold and distributed amongst NZ's people - contentious to this day!)

Named after the Viceroy of India at the time (George Eden - Earl of Auckland) it's original Maori name was Tamaki-makau-rau, which translates to Tamaki with a hundred lovers, which is acknowledgement of the fertile lands that surround the area (not an adulterer who didn't know how to be faithful).

This city is most likely the one you will arrive at from your long trip from overseas. It is affectionately called the city of sails, due to its close proximity to water and the many sailing ships that use its waters. The America's Cup (which is a world sailing trophy), has previously been competed for here. If New Zealand ever holds this trophy, and the competition is being sailed, make sure you head to the viaduct to take in all the action (It is at the time of writing in 2017, holder of the "Auld Mug". To see if your trip will correspond to any related events, visit http://emirates-team-new-zealand.americascup.com/

Connecting Auckland to its surrounding northern suburbs is just one bridge. Unfortunately that same bridge is the only way to access the top quarter of the North Island. For this reason, make sure you plan your trip accordingly. Do not get caught in rush hour traffic trying to get across unless you like being stuck in a car for long periods of time. If travelling up to the top of the North Island, from Auckland, avoid both 6-9am and 3-6pm. Likewise if travelling South from visiting the tip of the North Island, the same rules apply. The first and last days of public holidays are also horrendous, so try and avoid travelling on these days.

In terms of fun things to do (keeping in mind I don't know your capabilities as an athlete), riding or roller-blading along the shoreline from mission bay towards downtown can be a fun experience, as the path hugs the harbor and gives great views of Rangitoto Island and the harbor. If however you are more in the mood for a bit of wine tasting, then why not head to Waiheke Island (it was good enough for Lady Ga Ga to holiday on when she visited). It also has some good hikes and is easily accessible via the ferry that leaves from downtown Auckland, which allows you to bring your car if you are so inclined.

Now for the specifics
Auckland has a plethora (I have always enjoyed using that word) of walks and views. Utilizing the wisdom of my local friends, the following suggestions for awesome days were suggested.

Takapuna Beach

The walk along the coastline from Takapuna beach to Milford is high on the list. At the time of this writing, the best restaurant pre or post walk is the "Tok Tok" which is right near Takapuna beach. The walk is a great excuse simply to have lunch at a nice restaurant as it only takes 60 minutes one way, but is laced with history which you can decide if it's worth your time by visiting

The Hillary Track

Should you want to venture out of Auckland and head to the West Coast (on your way to places further north which are featured in more detail a little later), Bethells beach has a great walk with spectacular scenery called the Hillary track. For those who don't know, Sir Edmund Hillary was a New Zealander who was the first person in the world (along with Tenzing Norgay) to summit Mount Everest and survive.   A number of places throughout NZ reference him.

The Hillary track is a long one and something that can be completed over a couple of days, however, one can also do sections of the walk.

One of these sections starts at Bethells beach and climbs its way to Murawai beach in about 5-6 hours (take home: it's going to be a full day). The pathway is the Te Henga walkway section of the Hillary trail and will follow the coast line, across spectacular cliffs and rugged west coast beaches. As with any hike in New Zealand, one should come prepared with warm clothes and plenty of food and water. There are cafes located at Murawai beach so that you can have a reward for making it halfway. Murawai beach has parking as well, so you would be able to do the walk from either direction. Be sure to read the track info before heading out. It can be found at:

http://regionalparks.aucklandcouncil.govt.nz/hillary-trail/d7895956-d8dd-4931-9f26-1019b2d7e2fa

The surfing on these beaches is also world class, so if this is something you are into, then maybe a walk AND a surf is in order.

Kayak to Rangatoto

Nothing is more quintessentially kiwi than being on the water paddling to an island, and this locals suggestion was rated the #1 thing to try when visiting Auckland by the local papers. This catered trip will have you paddling across the harbor to an island, and served dinner whilst you watch the sun move its way to the horizon with Auckland's city lights in the background.

It is considered a paddle that anyone from beginner to expert can complete and is made even more amazing by the fact, you will be coming back during darkness to be in awe of the city at night. Just be sure to partner up with a fit paddler so that you can get lots of rest on the way back and then blame the tidal currents when they wonder why it suddenly got so hard.

If you are not already convinced, then why not check out the website and their reviews. Sounds like an amazing time to me.

Shakespear park

Most people wish to experience a combination of things when coming to NZ. The hope to see the lush green farm land, maybe a few sheep, stroll along some beaches and maybe take a few hikes. Well if that's your goal and you want to take it all in, on one day trip, then Shakespear park is for you.

Located just 40 minutes north of central Auckland, this park which doubles as a farm is sure to impress. With ample places to park your car, you can even camp overnight with your motor home (site availability of 30), or tent by visiting this website and clicking on park facilities

With its trails set amongst farm land, the more adventurous hiker can discover beautiful beaches and amazing views whilst sucking in the fresh sea air.

Russell

New Zealand's starting point, but scenery is where this stands out

Pronounced: If you can't pronounce this one, I'm afraid I can't help you

Named after: Lord John Russell.

Why you should go there: Beautiful landscapes, small town feel, a great place to spend the night whilst travelling north

This is a must see trip. To get there you will have to drive North of Auckland which as mentioned previously, has only one bridge to get you there. For this reason, don't be travelling that direction after 3pm, nor on a public holiday, unless your dream vacation involves being stuck in the car for 3 extra hours.

Once over the bridge, do yourself a favor, and take the toll road through the tunnel. To buy a toll pass simply pull into the service station, which is conveniently located just before the toll section, and buy a return pass, along with some car snacks to see you right. This is the fastest way to pay for the tolls if you have limited time.

Mungawai Heads is a great spot to enjoy

Once through the tunnel, start to look for the coastal roads that will be on your right hand side. These will travel away from the highway. You will pass beautiful beaches and small coastal towns, each of which are worth stopping at. As a starting point, Mungawai heads is where I tend to travel through and then simply follow the road along the coast. Waipu Cove and Langs beach all offer beautiful sandy beaches, which are very low key and therefore quiet. The best thing, is that because of the Queens chain, the beaches are open for everyone's use (refer to the 1st chapter if you skipped that one).

To get to Russell you will need to take the ferry. Whatever you do, don't be like me, and take the alternative long way, thinking the road less travelled will save you some money and provide undiscovered views.

Having been the victim of this decision once, it becomes clear as you pass by a farmer's fence which has over 500 hubcaps on it (I am deadly serious), that this road is a car's nemesis.

This dirt road, is rutted and sure to help those hubcaps off your car, and if you are like me, you will also have to contend with locals coming the other direction, on a road that seems to be designed to hold just one car at a time. By the time you get to Russell you would have been shaken more than a cocktail from your favorite bar tender and, more than likely, your travelling party will vote you out from behind the driver's wheel.

If that doesn't convince you, then I should also point out that the ferry ride is spectacular and is not long (although the wait to get on the ferry with your car can be).

The township of Russell is fantastic. Being the first place New Zealand held its government (well technically it was Okaito just down the road where the ferry stops) its feeling is very colonial. In its early years, the area was a lawless town with regular fights and prostitution. It is now the complete opposite, calm and welcoming, the ideal place to start a trip around the Bay of Islands.

There are many great houses one can stay in or bed and breakfasts, and if this is out of your price range, then the local camping ground is well maintained and extremely family orientated (there is however a strict no noise after 10pm policy - and I mean strict!). It is extremely busy around NZ's public holidays and if booking on Air bnb or VRBO, the places often require a minimum three night stay.

This view is from the main promenade of Russell. One of the many reasons to visit

For a great day at the beach, simply head over the back of the township to Oneroa Bay (pronounced ON - E - ROWER) where you will find great swimming and a calm beach perfect if you are travelling with kids (but not ideal if you are looking to surf).

One thing New Zealand is known for, is its lack of viscous wildlife and the many birds it has. This should not be interpreted to mean the birds won't cause you grief however. If you are in Russell you should still be cautious of one of New Zealand's rare birds, the Weka. To give you some idea of what you could awaken to, do not make the following mistake, as we did whilst camping there. Having left some open bread in our tent, we were awoken to said Weka (which are the size of a large rooster but look nothing like them), trying to grab a loaf of bread inside our tent at 5 in the morning. After all parties (including the Weka) screamed and ran around trying to get away from each other, the day's lunch was absconded with by this flightless bird, and the entire campground was able to start the day much earlier than they had planned…. Need I say more. Rare bird sighting check, wide awake from adrenaline check, and no lunch thanks to a greedy bird.

Russell is the perfect detour if you are trying to make your way up North to the better known tourist attractions of ninety mile beach, the tip of the North Island and the Kauri forests (which by the way are all very awesome). To access more information on this, there are plenty of websites and travel books that cater to those ideas.

Coromandel Peninsula

When all you feel like is a Sunday drive

Named after: Believe it or not, this area was named after a ship of the British Navy (the HMS Coromandel) after it entered the nearby harbor to get kauri spars (a type of tree that is throughout the area).

Why you should go: Glorious beaches, spectacular oceans, untouched paradise

This is a must drive for viewing rugged NZ coastline. If you travel to the town of Thames (not worth stopping in of itself unless restocking for your next adventure) and then continue up the coastline, you will drive a rugged remote coastline with sea views most of the way. With only small rural towns on this road, you can really get the feel for how NZ remains untouched in many places. If you are trying to make it to beaches such as cooks and hot water beach (mentioned in the Kawhia chapter), then it is possible to navigate around the whole peninsula. Just remember, the roads of New Zealand are very curvy, so if someone in your group is prone to car sickness, then regular stops and lots of time are the order of the day.

The Estuary at half tide. The perfect place for a paddle in a zen like location.

Whangamata

Small town meets great beach - get your paddle on

Pronounced (fonga martaa);

Meaning: The area comes from the M ā ori words 'whanga', which means bay, and 'mat ā ', which means a hard stone. The hard stone is in reference to a volcanic glass called obsidian, which is rare in these parts now, but occasionally can be discovered washed up on the beach.

Why you should go: Safe swimming, unique seafood, low key surf town, surfing mecca

This place is a great town to be at. At its busiest in the weekend and public holidays, it has one of NZ's safest beaches to swim at and has one of the best surf breaks NZ has to offer ("the bar at Whangamata" - does not refer to a place to drink in this instance although there is a pub if you are interested in that too). Short on good restaurants to eat at, resign yourself to fish and chips or a night out at the one good family owned and run restaurant (at least at the time of this writing) called Argo's. The seafood platter features locally caught seafood and is amazing. The restaurant menu can be found at this link: http://www.argorestaurant.nz

The town has a main street with numerous shops (think small coastal -not large coastal), along with a supermarket (it is a new world and is behind the main street close to the skateboard park). Since a number of activities mentioned in this section require you to know when high tide is, the easiest way to know when this is, is to get a free copy of the "Coastal News" which is available at local dairy's (better known as a minimart in North America) or newsagent's . This will also have the added benefit of listing upcoming events in the township and give you a sense of what the area has to offer from a community point of view. Conversely you can always consult this website http://www.metservice.com/marine-surf/tides/whangamata for tide times.

Long walks along the beach your kind of thing - Whanga delivers!

Whangamata's beach stretches for over 2km. It can be accessed from the many public entry points and has a harbor at one end, and an estuary at the other. These public entry points are easily marked by a white wooden posts and usually have a road leading toward them for easy access.

Whangamata was voted in 2018 as the best beach of New Zealand by readers of the national newspaper *"the New Zealand Herald".* Its popularity stems from its safe swimming beaches, awesome walkability, numerous activities, great café's, and ease of getting around, it is easy to see why this beach stood out amongst the hundreds New Zealand has to offer.

Treasure Island

If you want more than just a long walk along the beach then this next idea is for you. Wait until low tide and cross over to the big island (Clarke Island) that looks like it is completely surrounded by water.

Don't be fooled though, simply walking out to it, across from where the beach is turning a sharp corner, you will travel up to your thighs across a sandbar that is formed by the ocean currents (I repeat, do this only at LOW TIDE).

Once over the other side, there is a sheltered beach, and if you get really adventurous (be warned it's very steep with no guard railing up the top), you can walk to the top of the island on a non marked track which entry point is at the back of the beach on the island (another locals only bit of knowledge). Make sure you travel across to the Island before low tide is reached as if you spend too long there (say an hour after the tide has turned), you will find yourself either swimming, or waiting to be rescued (I have personally had to save tourists before). Whilst you cannot walk completely around the base of the Island, one can scramble across rocks and see crabs scurrying away. The water at the beach part of the island is also safe to swim in and can be a great place to go for a swim if travelling with kids.

Surfing/body boarding

If surfing is your thing and you are good enough to want to surf one of the best breaks in the world, then Whangamata delivers. "The Bar" is located at the harbor mouth on the far end of the "main beach". It fools many new comers to the area as when they go to surf, it doesn't appear to be working. This is because "The Bar" is a sand break and only works during low tide.   With hollow tubes and a fairly easy paddle out, it is popular amongst locals including Ella Williams, who is on the women's professional tour, and also works at her dad's surf shop in summer on the main street of Whanga (she is really friendly and nice, and is more than happy to sign autographs and take pictures with those who want them).

If "The Bar" seems a little intense for you, then there are many more relaxed breaks along the main beach and these work best at high tide. Next to the surf club is a surf lesson operation and if this isn't working, then a visit to the local surf shops on the main street will ensure you get your chance to say you surfed, by renting a board from them.

Paddleboarding

The Estuary: This beautiful area of Whangamata is best enjoyed at high tide (see photo at beginning of chapter). Paddle Boards can be rented at the local estuary store (which is also a great place to get fish and chips). If you are with little ones, or someone not so confident, there is also the option to rent kayaks. This is very much a "do it yourself" operation in that you will need to walk the paddle boards or kayaks to the estuary, but that is what makes NZ so low key.

The best time to do this is an hour before the high tide time. Paddle up the estuary away from the ocean mouth with the current (provided you do this before high tide time). Paddle as far as you feel like going (it goes a long way) and then meander back with the tide as it turns to go back out. Unless you want to feel like a hamster on a wheel, this is best done on a calm day, as when it gets windy, you can end up finding it very hard to make any progress.

The Harbor: Definitely a different experience than the estuary, it is once again best done at high tide before the tide turns (you can tell which direction the tide is going as the moored boats face against the direction of the water). I did this one year on a kayak and out of no-where, a pod of dolphins swam up the harbor with my wife and I. One of the best experiences I have ever had. Whilst I can't guarantee dolphins, the scenery and the paddling is awesome and if you get a little tired, you are able to stand on the harbor floor provided you are not still in the channel. I would recommend not trying this on a windy day as you will find it very hard to make any progress and could find yourself stuck at one end of the harbor having to walk back. Kayaks would be the better option if you still want to try this. The best place to rent paddle boards is from surfs up and if you want a guided tour to the magnificent donut island (named for the cave one enters to an open middle and pristine like view), then this is the crew for you.

Shellfish

Tua tua's are a local shellfish and are worth trying just once to say you did. When collecting them, leave them in fresh water overnight in a bucket before cooking (out of the sun) as you want encourage them to spit out the sand.

One very typical kiwi way of eating them is simply to boil them until their shells open (never eat any shellfish whose shells don't open after being cooked), and then drenching them in malted vinegar. Very tasty!

So how does one find said tua tua's? I hear you ask.

At low tide simply go out to the depth of your calves, wiggle your feet and sooner or later you will feel what seem to be rocks underneath your toes. Bend down, pull them out of the sand. **Make sure you throw back any tua tuas that are smaller than the length of a medium sized adult thumb as this allows the population to rejuvenate**.

Each person is allowed to take a small bucket a day from the ocean, but one bucket will easily feed a group. Most people will only want to eat a few.

The best places to look for these tend to be in front of the surf club on the main beach, or on Otahu beach to the right of the two big rocks when facing out toward the ocean (remember it has to be low tide).

Another note, be sure to check that it is okay to eat the tua tua's as there can be times during the year, that it is not advisable.   Typically this occurs in the summer months resulting in too much bacteria in the water which the shellfish filter to get their food and as a result accumulate the bacteria.   It can make you sick eating them and the best way to check is to go to the information place next to the library on the main street.

The other great thing to use tua tua's for is bait for fishing.

The Estuary is a great place to fish at low tide if you are introducing your children to the sport.

For the more serious fishermen there are fishing trips with bigger operations located down by the wharf (which are booked at the information center next to the library on the main street of Whangamata).

Popular events at Whangamata

- Whanga Week: Run by the surf club, this is an athletes paradise. Take part in many different running races, swimming events, and for the less competitive, there are organized walks to enjoy
- Beach Hop : Want to see old cars made new again and enjoy a big party in the process. This is your event! Watch as old cars from the 50's and 60's drive around town turning Whanga into a historic postcard. This event is big so expect it to be busy.
- Brits at the beach: Are you from the British Isles? Then if you wish to connect to your homeland, this is the place to do it.

Whiritoa

Blowholes and seclusion, walk it out

Pronounced: fairy tow a

Meaning: weaving warrior.

Why you should go: Undiscovered beaches and blowholes

Trust me this is not a beach you want to swim at. With a steep shoreline, the backwash is powerful and can knock an inexperienced swimmer off their feet and out to sea fairly quickly.

So why would I suggest visiting this potential death trap? There is visual gold to be discovered here in the form of a secluded beach and a blowhole.

Whiritoa Blowhole

At one end of the beach (the south end) lies the blow hole. Check this out and you will see the force of nature at its best and true to kiwi form, there is no fence to prevent you from falling in, so be sure to be careful. It is located at the southern end of the beach and requires hiking up a somewhat steep trail. The best time to see this is probably at high tide due to the need for the water to hit it at a certain angle. Either way, it is great for a day hike as Waimama Bay lies at the other end of the beach. For further information on both walks, the following website gives great additional detail.

Waimama Bay

At the other end of the beach, lies a meandering stream, which if you cross it, and walk along the bush line, towards the houses, you will come to path (it looks like a hidden track). The path begins walking up hill through a beach side forest which is relatively well maintained. Once through the bush line you will then follow the fence line next a farm which will eventually lead to a beautiful vista of several bays. Finally it will weave down to a secluded beach with rock pools and a relatively safe beach to swim at.

Unless you know someone in this area, you will not know this exists (the price you paid for this book was worth it for this piece of info alone!).

As with all things concerning water (and in particular the ocean), never turn your back to the sea, even on what seems like a safe place on the rocks. There is always potential for a rogue wave to come through and sweep you into the sea. (little known fact - rock fishing is one of the most dangerous sports in the world due to this occurrence)

Onemana

Tennis and hiking. Another great beach

Pronounced: o knee marna

Why you should go: Tennis courts with the best view, unknown hikes

If you are a tennis player and have the kids with you, you can tick two boxes with this secret oasis. With the best view in town, the tennis courts at the beach are free to use and right next to a playground. Childcare problem solved, beautiful view, the secrets keep expanding.

There is even a cafe right next door if you feel like doing coffee afterwards.

If tennis isn't your thing, then there is a long hike, which will take you to several secluded beaches along the coastline. The walk begins at the top of the hill. Simply continue driving past the tennis courts and follow the road to the top. There is also a place to park your car. The walk will take you to several secluded beaches along a narrow pathway with spectacular coastal views. The pathway becomes quite narrow and steep in parts but you were after something that not everybody was going to be at right? For this reason, please make sure you are capable of scaling some steep terrain. You will get spectacular farm views and ocean views throughout the walk to reward your efforts.

For this reason alone, Onemana is worth the visit.

This isolated beach is one of three that you can access from the hike

For a more detailed overview of this amazing hike with great beaches, visit this website for more thorough directions.

http://www.whangamatanz.com/onemana-south-coastal-reserve.html

Opoutere

Secluded long beach connected to an inlet AND easy to get to.

Pronounced: o pooh tiri

Meaning: Place of floating posts.

Why you should go: Secluded harbor town, untouched beach, explorer's paradise

Don't let the name fool you, this undiscovered piece of paradise is far from a log laden harbor. Its history involves gum diggers, gold diggers and logging, all of which have long disappeared.

This side town slightly off the beaten track will ensure a fun excursion. After driving past the batches of the area (which were built in the early 1950's and 60's), and the harbor, take a left turn at the signpost indicating Opoutere beach. Once past the backpackers, you will come to Ohui road. At this junction take a sharp right and you have arrived at the car park. From there take a 10 minute walk through the pine trees and experience a New Zealand beach, yet to be altered by man's hands.

The long beach stretching over 5km one direction enables an awesome walk and as not many people come by, you could easily find yourself all alone with no one in sight. Strike yogi pose, namastee!

(other amenities are limited, so bring supplies!)

For a slightly more detailed overview, this website will give you general directions on how to get there

If you are in Whangamata, you have two options of where to travel next. One takes you to Hamilton, the other to a different beach side city called Tauranga. For the purposes of simplicity, I am going to suggest going through Hamilton (it's not a tourist mecca), but if you still feel the urge to go through Tauranga, be sure to walk up Mount Maunganui and get an amazing view of the surrounding beaches. The walk is a tough slog uphill with lots of stairs, for around 40 minutes, but the view is spectacular. Once again, there are no safety fences so keep this in mind when climbing up the mountain.

Waikino Gorge

If you go back through Hamilton from Whangamata you will drive through the Waikino gorge which is located just outside Waihi, and is the site of old gold mines. It is also where one can take a fairly flat ride along a long bike path that is off the main road, with no cars. It is a fabulous way to explore some of the tunnel systems and old mining sites that are littered throughout the valley. It is suitable for all ages and is a great way to enjoy a leisurely afternoon when you are just wanting to break up the trip you are taking. The trail follows what used to be a train line and has views of a meandering stream through the gorge where a big industrial gold mining operation used to exist in the early 1900's.

If you do not have a bike then the station has been converted into an old school cafe/restaurant and they rent the bikes for half a day or a full day. It is best to call ahead as there is a limited supply. Conversely you can also rent bikes from a bike hire service for around 45 dollars an hour. Visit https://nzbybike.com/regions/coromandel/paeroa/hauraki-rail-trail-bike-hire-and-shuttle/

On the other side of this gorge (which is possible to ride your bike to along the rail trail), is the town of Paeroa. This town is famous for one thing. The big L&P replica bottle on the main road. If one was to taste an original drink in NZ, this would be the place to do it. L&P soft drink combines mineral water from local springs with a lemonade ice block taste and is something that you will only find in this part of the world. Not to mention, it is delicious.

Hamilton

Best just for the rest stop it provides and maybe lunch.

Why you should go there: Refuel, dine well, enjoy the river.

This city is a central travel through point in the North Island, that to be honest, I would not rate as a tourist mecca. However, by the time most travelers are driving through, a break is in order and you might as well do something.

So, with this in mind, a great way to get fresh air and enjoy a walk would be to visit the Hamilton botanical gardens and walk along the Waikato river. The gardens are large and for those of you travelling with kids, it has a playground. There is also a cafe with reasonable food.

For those wanting a bit more in the way of restaurants, the southern end of Victoria St (what can I say, the queen was very influential in these parts) has a number of options which should cater to most people's tastes. The city itself is not a shopping mecca, but in the aptly named Centreplace (downtown Hamilton), there are a number of shops that will help in restocking the wardrobe whilst on your trip. Another area that is popular among the locals, is "The Base"

If you are in search of a bigger play area for the kids, then Hamilton lake (more like a pond compared to those of North America), is a great place to keep them entertained, and it does have a walkway that goes completely around it. This can also be a great place for a picnic on route to the next destination and it does have a cafe that serves food.

Waitomo

CAVES AND CAVING - This couldn't get more real!

Pronounced: Why tomo

Meaning: Water passing through a hole. (very inventive I know)

Why you should go: Spectacular holes, spiritual experience, adrenaline potential

The Waitomo Caves

These caves are perhaps one of the most famous tourist locations in New Zealand, due to the extensive cave system throughout the area and the glow worms that reside within them.

The caves are an absolute must see. However avoid the tourist trap. To be clear, the tourist trap is the small cheaper cave where tourist bus after bus, comes by and gives people the chance to say they saw some glow worms - yipppeee!.

Sure it has glow worms and you can say you ticked the box, but the real impressive caves that cost more to see are worth the investment. The Ruakuri caves will take you deep into the bowels of the earth, with a guide and a safe walking track (fine for children). Here you will see massive Stalactites and Stalagmites, glow worms and hear about the significance the area has to the Maori. The highlight for me, and hopefully you, is feeling the noticeable temperature change as you walk near an ancient burial ground, very crazy and unexplainable. Attached is the link to the official website which has up to date pricing and times of the tour. For the record, you should make sure to book in advance as these tours can sell out. Don't leave it to the last minute or you may be disappointed.

http://www.waitomo.com/ruakuri-cave/Pages/default.aspx

Want to go even more crazy? How about BLACK WATER tubing?

Rappel down into a dark cave and then take a flying fox to add to the adrenaline rush before entering the slow moving fresh water within the cave system. This trip gets cold, but with hot chocolate provided you'll stay relatively warm as you float on an inner tube into the open (you are provided with wetsuits as well!).

If you really want to push your limits, ask your guide to take you through the caving exit where you will actually have to squeeze through a small tight caving system and climb out via a small sloping waterfall. It really feels authentic so don't do it if you suffer from sever claustrophobia.

This tour will last about 5 hours and is in water about 10 degrees Celsius. It is by far the best way to experience the caves, simply because you get it all. Glow worms, caving and heaps of fun. Yes the price is a little bit more crazy ($240NZ at the time of writing), but you did say you wanted the least known tourist experiences whilst still doing things that only NZ can provide.http://www.waitomo.com/black-water-rafting/Pages/black-abyss.aspx

Kawhia beach

You want remote and special, this beach is it

Pronounced: car fi a

Meaning: Abundance of everything.

Why you should go: Remote location, unique experience, great for the muscles

This beach has a significant connection to the Maori people of NZ due to it being the original landing place of the Tainui people when they first visited NZ.   Aside from this significance, it also holds a locals secret that you are now about to have shared with you.

Everyone who goes to New Zealand is told about the hot water beach sand pools that exist at hot water beach (obvious name given the context).

This is a fantastic opportunity and many tourist operations can give you that experience. If however you are the more adventurous traveler and would prefer this experience to be one only a few people know about, then you must go to Kawhia. It is remote (be warned, it may feel like you are getting lost) and if you like to be on a rugged beach soaking in hot water from a volcanic fault line, then this is your trip.   Make sure you go at LOW TIDE as this is the only time the sand will be exposed without being under the surf. This beach is unpatrolled (meaning no lifeguards) and has some rip currents in the surf, so resist the temptation to go swimming above your knees after your hot water soak (plus it's cold anyway).

MAKE SURE TO BRING A GOOD QUALITY SPADE: Don't bring a cheap plastic option if you want to truly enjoy this experience. Follow the directions from the website I have provided below and make your way down to where the water would usually be at high tide. Take your awesome metal spade and start digging. It may take a couple of tries as there are only certain sections of the beach that these exist, but you will know you have the right place as the water is unmistakably hot and you can feel it coming up to the surface!

For more information on how to get there and where to dig, check visit the website

http://www.nzhotpools.co.nz/hot-pools/kawhia-springs-te-puia-springs/

As this is for the more adventurous traveler, I wanted to provide you with one of the reviews "just as good as hot water beach without the line-up of tourist buses". Once again, you're welcome

Rotorua

See the mud pools, but once that's done, time to ride

Pronounced: roto roo a

Meaning: second lake

Why you should go: Biking bonanza, volcanic activity, bouncing ball action.

This region is going to stink!!!! Sulfur spurts from the ground practically everywhere you look. It is probably the most visited tourist destination in New Zealand and is where you can see Maori cultural displays and mud pools.

By all means check out the cultural center as the people working there are legitimately doing the work of a proud culture. However there are many other lesser known tourist spots that are well worth checking out.

The blue lakes: Take a drive over small hill (or better yet, bike it from the Rotorua mountain bike center (you can walk it as well) and see the most amazingly beautiful blue lake. This one is okay to swim in (not all of them are due to sulfuric acid issues) and is a great place to cool off. Down the road is the buried village, which could be okay for a look but in terms of the premise of this book it is too well known and is a popular tourist attraction. If history is your thing, then it will meet this need as an eruption buried the entire village in volcanic fallout preserving it for all to see.

Rotorua mountain bike center

If you have ever wanted to Mountain bike, then this place is one of the meccas. Rated one of the world's hotspots by velogear ride advisor, it caters to all levels of riders, from novice to crazy nutball.

With trails marked beginner, intermediate and advanced, there is some awesome fun to be had cruising through beautifully aged forests and well maintained tracks that can be as long or as short as you like. Travelling through the Whakarewarewa trail network is akin to being in the lord of the rings bush (no it wasn't in the movie) on a bike.

Don't have a bike? That is also taken care of thanks to the many bike shops around the location.

What makes this even more awesome is that the trails are free to use for everybody.

Any other excuses?

Well I think a ride is in order, don't you?

As there are so many trails the best thing to do is visit the website before arriving and making a plan on what ride you will do. I have placed two links to give you many options. The redwoods link has a more comprehensive overview of the area catering to all levels of riders. Ride Rotorua focuses more on the different serious mountain biker options.

http://redwoods.co.nz/bike/

http://www.riderotorua.com/index.php

If being on a bike isn't everyone in your party's cup of tea, then there are also many walking trails near the center. Here is a word to the wise, take it from my poor form, best not to challenge those novices with your group to join you on the harder rides, you may put them off riding forever… just ask my wife.

http://redwoods.co.nz/walk/

Want to roll down the hill in a big inflatable ball? No? Maybe your kids? This is the place it got invented.   Might as well give it a go for a laugh, you will only be here once right? The prices are a little steep, but from what the photos show, it looks like it could be well worth the fun. There are two options in Rotorua and both are listed below along with photos so you can get a better idea of what to expect.

http://ogo.co.nz/prices.html

https://www.zorb.com

The Tongariro Crossing

It's not one of the 10 best voted hikes in the world for nothing

Pronounced: Tong a rare ro

Meaning: The word tongariro literally means, "I am borne away in the bitter south wind", and comes from an ancient Maori folklore.

Why you should go: The challenge, the beauty, the bragging rights, oh and the barn

Recently added as a world heritage site, it has great significance to the Maori people and is consistently voted as one of the top ten hikes in the world to do.

Be warned this is a 20km hike across really tough terrain, which includes scaling boulders and walking down loose scree. However, my 7 year old completed it, thanks to a lot of encouragement and offers of big ticket rewards towards the end (such as video games and sugar treats). The take home on this, is, that if you are reasonably fit and have done some longer hikes you should be fine, I just wouldn't do it if the longest hike your family has ever done is 2km.

Given that most people start hiking early in the morning, you are going to want to stay near the walk. The best place based on our visit is on airbnb called "The Barn" (which for this portion of the book counts as secret knowledge as everyone knows about the hike). The hosts, who are not paying me any money to say this, are awesome. Their converted barn sleeps a whole party of 12 and if you want smaller accommodation they have that as well. If you really want to get adventurous, then there is the self-sustaining environmentally friendly tree house. Ask them also about the bathtub in the woods, which they will light a fire under to heat the water and give you a truly authentic kiwi hot tub experience. You will however have to provide your own bubbles (I am referring to sparkling wine to those of you who were wondering).

The setting is amazing, with no houses to block the awesome view and plenty of farmland, it is one of the most authentic kiwi stays I have had and very peaceful.

Booking a shuttle to get you to the start of the walk is essential. The walk is one way and so if you don't have two cars, you will be stuck on the other side of the mountain. The shuttle will take you to the start of the walk and then get you at the end. You can arrange to have it pick you up from the barn, but it will cost less if you simply drive 10 minutes down the road to meet it at the starting point of the shuttle service. Be prepared to wake up early to start this trip as the hike is a good 7 hours. You will need to pack warm clothes that allow for the potential of snow, wind and driving rain, along with good food and lots of water (there is nowhere to drink on the way). For this reason, try and pack layers so as not to weigh your bag down with heavy clothing. The first half of the hike is quite steep and is only made harder if you are carrying a heavy backpack.

The hike is very popular but never feels crowded due to the vastness of the landscape. The Mountain was made famous for its appearance in the movie Lord of the Rings, where it was known as Mount Doom. Since you are not in a movie, the real name is Mount Ngauruhoe
 and yes it is volcanic (although it hasn't erupted in some time).

Another word to the wise is that toilets are at a premium in this place, so when you see one, whether you feel like going or not - go! The landscape is as bare as a bum, so if you don't want yours seen by hundreds of onlookers, you best take the opportunity whilst you got it.

Another critical point is you must bring all your own supplies and as such must also take with you any garbage (read: no rubbish bins along the route). This is hiking at its best, which means very little impact from mankind (aside from the hundreds trekking it).

Finally, as the translation suggests, this trail is very prone to changes in weather. Plan your trip accordingly. Pack lots of different clothes for the weather and aim to hike this in summer when the chances of good weather are at their best. Once the mountain closes in, it can be very hard to see where one is and even more importantly, the spectacular views. A case in point was a tourist we met on the way who had to turn back on a previous trip. He had met a lone hiker who said he was lucky to be alive due to not being able to see where he was going further up the mountain. Bottom line, if the weather's not cooperating, best leave it to another time or you could find yourself questioning your choice.

Mount Ngauruhoe and the Tongararo crossing. Just some of the amazing scenes you will see on this climb

Whanganui

This river connects the people to the land. Best paddle it

Pronounced: Fong a noo eee

Meaning: There are two stated meanings for one of New Zealand's oldest cities and the river that flows to it. Big harbor is one and long wait is the other.

If cruising through ancient forests steeped in ancient folklore whilst sleeping under the stars sounds like your cup of tea, then read on!

Kayak/Canoe Trip

Being one of New Zealand's longest navigable waterways, the Wanganui river runs from Mt Tongariro (which you just read about), to the ocean. Given this fact, it would stand to reason that this would be the perfect river to kayak.

This experience is something that most people can experience through a guided canoe trip. Its remoteness and ruggedness is bound to help you leave the city stresses of life far behind, and get you in touch with New Zealand's rugged nature. Added bonus, you are getting fit at the same time! For a great 3 day version of the paddle (there are 4 and 5 day trips as well), then try the Whakahoro to Pipiriki section. The trip includes food and accommodation along the river complete with a guide to give you the history of the area. If you are looking for something a little more unique that the average tourist bus doesn't visit then you are in the right spot.

Now before you start wondering if you could do it, or if you will need to navigate raging rapids, my 65 year old mother and father pulled it off, and seemed to indicate it wasn't too hard. So don't wonder if it's possible, just book the thing.

To get prices and tee up your trip with the company they raved about, click the following link.

http://www.whanganuirivercanoes.co.nz/our-prices

New Plymouth

Spectacular accommodation meets rugged coastline and ability to ski and surf in one day

This awesome city is a good one to make part of your drive around NZ, especially if you are heading to either the Wairarapa or Wellington. With a large coastal walkway that is suitable for biking and plenty of surfing, it is unique in that you potentially could ski and surf in the same day (Mt Taranaki has a small ski hill).

One of the best reasons however, is accommodation that is just a few kilometers from the city center called Ahu Ahu Villas.

These chalets are situated 10 minutes' drive from the city of New Plymouth and are simply a spectacular place to sit and unwind as you watch the endless swells hit the beach. While this might be a bit more than you would normally spend on accommodation, the reward of the view makes it worthwhile.

To see the actual accommodation I am talking about the website is as follows

http://www.ahu.co.nz/

To book them through Airbnb, the listing is as follows

https://www.airbnb.ca/rooms/13513627?guests=2&adults=2&children=0&infants=0&location=new%20plymoth&s=BGDqL9vz

This place like many other places in NZ was discovered by my wife and I by chance. We simply called in at the information center (located in the city of New Plymouth) and were lucky enough to be rewarded. Of course this was before air bnb was even a baby, so don't take the chance and book before going.

With the windswept ocean as your viewpoint and the beach able to be walked to, this is sure to take romance to a whole new level.

If you are wanting a couple of things to do whilst in the area, then there is the botanical gardens which are tranquil and serene. If this isn't your thing, then the coastline has a path that stretches the length of the city of New Plymouth and is also the location of some great surfing. Great for those who like to stroll along the beach or get their feet wet

Now if one of your goals is to say that you skied and surfed all in one day, then rent yourself some skis in town and then head to the Mountain you can't miss. This cone shaped Mountain which also goes by the name of Mt Egmont is what New Plymouth is known for. Now this isn't your most amazing ski hill ever, but the chances of others ever being able to say they skied and surfed all in the same day are pretty slim.

http://skitaranaki.co.nz/SMC/

Martinborough

Wine and cheese, need I go on? Okay it has got some great views as well

Why you should go: Variety, ruggedness, tastiness and of course the wine!

Not to be confused with the great wine region of Marlborough, this wine region is typically only discovered when talking to locals (lucky for you, you bought this book). Located on the other side of the Rumatukas (the mountains behind Wellington), the central wine tasting shop has the some of the region's best wines that you honestly can't get anywhere else in the world.

Lake Ferry which is a short drive from the above accommodation has a really cool pub with a really non-descript extremely non fancy interior and at the time of this writing has an amazing chef. Good food, secret location, and beautifully remote, the secret is out. The only caveat to this piece of gold, is that I cannot control the chef's movements. At the time of writing this is accurate, but once again double check with the locals to be sure it is still considered a great place to eat. If nothing else, it will add to your adventure.

The following section is thanks to a personal connection to the media and is provided by the communications director of the region of Wairarapa. I asked her to provide details of the hidden gems that locals enjoy taking their visitors too. Take it from me, if anyone should know, what are the best things to do in this area, it is Katie.

View from the Palliser lighthouse

Putangirua Pinnacles

The Putangirua Pinnacles near Cape Palliser are some of the most amazing rock formations you will ever see. Put on your sturdy walking shoes and do a day trip, or bring the family camping here. This spot has star quality too – Sir Peter Jackson filmed here for The Lord of the Rings: The Return of the King. The pinnacles are an hour's drive south of Martinborough.

Nearby is Cape Palliser lighthouse with its red and white stripes. Being home to the largest seal colony in the North Island, it is a great place to get in touch with the wildlife of the area.

The Waiohine Gorge

The suspension bridge over the Waiohine River forms a spectacular gateway to the Tararua Forest Park and a sensational spot to get a great view of the Waiohine Gorge. This area, a 15 minute drive from

Greytown and Carterton, is an idyllic spot for family-friendly camping, swimming and short and long walks.

Castlepoint Beach and Lighthouse at its finest

Castlepoint Beach & Lighthouse

Spectacular Castlepoint is a 50 minute drive from Masterton. Here, is some of New Zealand's most jaw-dropping natural scenery including a limestone reef, imposing Castle Rock and lagoon and golden sand beach. To top it off, the lighthouse which has guarded over this coastline for more than 100 years. There are popular places to surf, fish and swim here and while a collection of "kiwi baches" (translate: holiday home) add to the holiday atmosphere.

Pukaha Mount Bruce Wildlife Centre

I threw this one in for something a little more family friendly. Most people when they come to NZ want a chance to see the famous Kiwi and as they are pretty hard to see in the wild, this may provide the opportunity you are looking for. I will acknowledge that this may not be the most exciting part of your visit, but will still provide some great scenery and the chance to learn about New Zealand's ecosystem.

This center, is a 20 minute drive north of Masterton. Pukaha is home to some of New Zealand's most rare and endangered wildlife including white Kiwi Manukura, who can be viewed in the Kiwi House alongside brown kiwi. Each day there is a Tuatara talk & feed (11.30am); eel feed (1.30pm) Kokako Talk (2.15pm) and Kaka Circus feed (3pm) while the new free flight aviary is a chance to see blue duck up close and easy to walk trails weave through lush native forest. The café serves great coffee while the interactive gallery with its rata tree full of creepy crawlies is for kids of all ages.

Beer and Wine: what else could be better?

The Wairarapa is perhaps New Zealand's best kept liquor secret. The region boasts many wineries and breweries which has garnered many awards. When travelling through this region, I tasted the best red that I have ever had. Due to my naivety of just how lucky I was to find such a great drop, I cannot recall which winery made such a fine drop. The only solution will be for you to visit and try and find it for yourself.

Tui Brewery

It may have a small population, but Mangatainoka certainly has a big reputation. The rural township nestled amongst the rolling hills of heartland New Zealand is home to legendary New Zealand beer label Tui and Tui HQ, which offers a visitor experience like no other. Here visitors can have lunch at the café and bar, buy from the retail shop selling quirky merchandise and catch up on their local history knowledge thanks to the small museum that tracks the site's 125 year-old history. A terrific garden bar complements the experience. For those who always wanted to see their name on a beer bottle, the tour offers you the chance to personalize your own beer (naturally this will cost you, but some might say its priceless).

Martinborough Brewery

Reward yourself with a cold craft beer made on site at the Martinborough Brewery after a day exploring the wine village of Martinborough. This industrial chic brewery is a popular spot, especially in the late afternoon sun. There are six varieties of beer brewed on site as well as a guest craft beer. Given all the active suggestions throughout this book, I figured you would need a day of to recuperate and what says recuperate better than drinking a cold one.

Wine tasting in Martinborough

The wine village of Martinborough, only one hour's drive or train ride from Wellington, is the perfect getaway for wine and food aficionados. Named after Irish immigrant John Martin, who in a gesture of patriotism laid the town out like a Union Jack and named the streets after foreign cities he'd visited. Martinborough has long been a service town for the south Wairarapa. But in 1980, on the back of a government report which suggested the soil and climate had very good potential for vineyards, the area transformed itself into a premium wine growing region.

Today there are more than 20 boutique vineyards within walking or cycling distance to the town square. Because many vineyards produce handcrafted wines, it means visitors have a good chance of meeting the wine-maker face to face and hearing their story first hand.

Some recommended cellar doors include Poppies Martinborough, Ata Rangi, Cambridge Road, Palliser Estate and Luna. A number of these same wineries also provide food which is the ultimate win win for anyone looking for an awesome way to have lunch.

In the center of the town is a wine tasting center which features a number of these wineries all in one place. This is where I tasted the wine to beat all wines (I am still bitter that I didn't take a photo and it has been over 15 years since I had it). They also have some walking tours of the wineries where you can be guided to some of the best!

Food Forest Organics

This delicatessen sells 95 percent organic food and can be found in the historic Ballie House in the pretty colonial township of Greytown. Owned by Hollywood movie director James Cameron, who lives in the south Wairarapa, it sells fresh produce that comes direct from the Cameron Family Farm as well as walnut oil, hemp seed oil and honey.

If you want to check out the latest offerings, then this is the website of his business.

http://www.foodforestorganics.co.nz

Schoc Chocolate

Do a tasting at Greytown chocolate studio Schoc and discover more than 80 different flavors'. Owner Murray Langham believes chocolate is more savory than sweet so flavors' include cardamom, toasted sesame and strawberry & black pepper as well as perennial favorite's lime & chili and lemon white. Schoc is located in the super cute building next to Cobblestones Museum on the Main Street.

http://www.schoc.co.nz

Olivo Olive Grove

Olivo is the oldest commercial olive grove in the Wairarapa. Helen Meehan will tutor you through a tasting of her distinctive flavored infused oils including fennel, porcini, lemon and smoked paprika. Olivo is in Martinborough.

www.olivo.co.nz

C'est Cheese

New Zealand is known for its cheeses so if you are in the Wairararapa you would be remiss to miss C'est Cheese. If the quaint setting isn't enough for you, then the award winning cheeses should be the tipping point.

Cheese maker Paul Broughton has opened a sensational little shop in Featherston. Selling specialty cheeses made by 20 different producers, including locally made Kingsmeade and Cwmglyn, there is also a comprehensive and gorgeous range of cured meats, olive oil, chutneys, relishes, breads and more. Set in a stylish shop with a focus on local and craft made.

https://purewairarapa.co.nz/producers/cest-cheese/

Need to work off the food? Time to get on your bike!

Rivenrock Mountain Bike Park

Located on the outskirts of Carterton and Masterton, this is a purpose built and professionally designed mountain bike park based on a private 500 acre farm near Mount Holdsworth. Stage one opened in January 2017 and includes 12km of purpose built trails that weave through pine forest, farmland and also uses existing forestry trails. Over the coming years, Rivenrock owners The Hind Family are planning to add many more kilometers of tracks over their 500 plus acres of farmland.

Typically they are open only on the weekends but times can vary.

The benefit for you is this will not be in any other travel book as it is that new! All the reviews from riders, indicate that this is one of those hidden gems. If this sounds like your cup of tea then visit their facebook page.

https://www.facebook.com/pg/rivenrockmtb/about/?ref=page_internal

Riding the Rimutaka Cycle Trail

The Rimutaka Cycle Trail goes through New Zealand's capital city Wellington and neighboring Wairarapa. It offers the perfect opportunity to mix riding with culture, cuisine and shopping. It's the quintessential kiwi ride featuring all types of New Zealand landscape: a river valley, bush-clad mountains, lake-sides, farm land and a rugged coast.

Beginning at Petone's Foreshore, the 115km Trail can be accessed by catching the train from Wellington Railway Station or by taking bikes on the East by West Ferry from Queen's Wharf. Nearby Jackson St, a popular and picturesque boulevard of boutiques, cafés, bars and restaurants, is the perfect place to grab a bite to eat and a locally roasted coffee before hitting the trail.

Here you will head north alongside the Hutt River on a well-defined cycle path, before heading through the Rimutaka Ranges via the historic railway route and enter the Wairarapa Valley at Cross Creek.

At this stage you will have a choice of turning left and following the 9km off-road limestone trail to Featherston where you can refuel and even learn about the historic tunnels you've just ridden through at The Fell Locomotive Museum, OR, you can turn right and head south, following the shore of Lake Wairarapa. The road weaves through rolling countryside, passed historic farms many of which offer accommodation and passed the turn-off to Wharekauhau Luxury Lodge where Prince William and Princess Katherine stayed during their 2014 Royal Tour of New Zealand.

At Ocean Beach you will be rewarded with views across Cook Straight (the stretch of ocean between the North Island and South Island) to the snow-capped mountains behind Kaikoura before weaving around the dramatic South Coast to the finish at Orongorongo. Here one can be met by Rimutaka Shuttles who make the trip out to the meeting point via Coast Road from Wainuiomata or by Green Jersey Cycle Tours who offer a range of guided or supported tours.

One of the best aspects of the Trail is its multiple access points meaning you can tailor the journey to suit your needs and fitness level. It can be completed in one day or done over two, three or four days, allowing for side trips to the wine village of Martinborough, the pretty colonial township of Greytown or out to NZ's first lighthouse at Pencarrow.

The following links will help plan this part of your trip.

http://www.nzcycletrail.com/trails/rimutaka-cycle-trail/ : This gives a great overview of what to expect on the ride. It also has further information on tour operators.

http://greenjersey.co.nz : This tour company offers multi day tours throughout the trail and also wine tours in the Martinborough region.

Wellington

Capital City with Culture.

Pronounced: as it sounds. You don't want me to patronize you I am sure.

Why you should go: Culture, Beer, Food and Scenery

Named after: Arthur Wellesley, who was able to defeat Napolean when he commanded the British, and was also the Prime Minister of Britain at one stage. Being the good servants of England that NZer's were, they named their capital city after him (remembering NZ's capital is Wellington is sure to help you win Trivia nights in other countries - most think it's Auckland).

Windy Wellington definitely lives up to its namesake. Based at the bottom of the North Island, it was recently named one of the best places on the planet to live (according to Duetche Bank 2017). It is also where you would catch a ferry across to Picton should you wish to extend your trip to the South Island.

Known in tourist circles, for the New Zealand national museum, Te Papa, it has many more things one can do. If you are at a loose end, Wellington is known as New Zealand's cultural capital of the New Zealand. Just by walking through the downtown you will see many shops offering custom made jewelry and art. Complete with great cafes and restaurants, this should be an area to check out if you want a great night out on the town.

The "Cake Tin" is Wellingtons local sport stadium and plays host to Super 12 rugby (the Hurricanes), NZ cricket, and the occasional All Black Rugby game. If you are in town when any of the above teams are playing, be sure to take in the atmosphere. It is like nothing else especially if the game is against Australia!

Here is what the locals seem to like doing.

Beer tours.

The following beer tour was suggested (mmm beeeeerrrrr) as best kept secret breweries that one must include on any beer tour.

Little Beer Quarter

Malthouse

Hashigo Zake and finally for good measure

Havana Bar just for fun (it actually doesn't serve much in the way of beer, just good music and a good time).

These are all within close walking distance to each other (look on the map before you go), and the Malthouse is right across from Te Papa (which is the New Zealand museum) so if you have some other people you know wanting to do that, they will at least know where to find you.

If beer isn't your thing, then I guess there is always the tram ride up to the botanical gardens (yes I know, this is also in many other books), but what makes this a little more awesome is the view you will get whilst riding the tram and also the fact you are riding New Zealand's only Funicular railway (yes it's a thing). If it doesn't sound that original at least you know that locals also recommend this as an activity to do.

No visit to New Zealand is complete without a photo taken in front of New Zealand's parliament. Better known as the "beehive" because of its remarkable resemblance to what a honey bee calls home, this hive of activity is set on a special moving platform to withstand the irregular earthquakes that occur due to the fault line that runs through the city.

The Weta Workshop

What about awesome movie scenes? Then why not visit the Weta workshop (Weta's are an insect that looks like something from the dinosaur area but are completely harmless). Not only did the locals I talked to suggest it's amazing, but when I looked at the reviews, there was nothing but 5 stars. There are many ways to see this, for the best option for your trip their website lists the many ways to enjoy this icon. Given that 5000 people a day go through this (and keep in mind it still has 5 star ratings), you will want to make sure you book in advance!

http://wetaworkshop.com/visit-us/workshop-tours/.

A Word About Hobbits

One of the most visited places in New Zealand is Hobbiton. For those of you unfamiliar with the movie *the lord of the rings*, there were characters called Hobbits that lived in a town. The movie set which hobbiton was shot at, is now a place one can visit on a farm in Matamatta. Now this might seem not that interesting to some, but by all accounts it is meant to be an amazing experience which culminates in having a drink at the hobbit pub that was featured in the movie.

So why am I telling you all this?

Simple really, the place gets over 3500 people A DAY! Bottom line, if you want to see it you need to book it advance, unless you like turning up to watch others go on a tour. More importantly, this applies to many other more popular attractions that New Zealand has to offer, so don't leave things to the last minute, be sure to book in advance. To help you out, here is the link so you have no excuses

https://www.hobbitontours.com/en/

The same goes for the Weta workshops that were mentioned in the previous chapter, with the exception that they get 5000 people through a day!.

You have been warned. Things get popular once the word is out!

If you are wondering how best to fit this into your trip, it is easily accessible on your way down the country from Hamilton, Whangamata or Tauranga. I have added it to the interactive map should you want to take a closer look. Good luck in your quest to protect the ring!

Final Words

New Zealand is a great place to explore with many amazing activities and people to meet. This book will take you off some of the more popular routes, and back onto them. There are plenty of other unique opportunities if you simply trust your instincts and ask locals, just like the ones I did for this book.

NZ relies heavily on tourism and nothing makes a kiwi happier than helping a person from a foreign land.

As you tour NZ, you are sure to find some other great experiences which will no doubt make you wonder why they are not in this book. I would love for you to share them with me so that I can continue to update this guide and give an even better experience for other readers. My email is timhoyster@gmail.com

Likewise, given I wrote this guide to bring as much enjoyment as possible for anyone going to NZ, I would love for you to send me photos of you in some of the places where I suggested you go (don't worry I won't publish them without your permission).

As with any guide, not all of the activities will live up to your personal expectations, but I hope on reflection, a good majority will and that this will make your experience of the North Island unique to you. If you found that some of the experiences I covered in this book didn't appeal, please let me know and more importantly, what it was about them that didn't appeal. Feedback is a gift and I welcome it even if it is pointing out improvements needed.

Thank you kind reader, I wish you the best trip ever through the North Island of NZ and look forward to hearing of the memories you created that will last you a lifetime

Map of New Zealand North Island with special access to Google Maps (hyperlinked)

Figure 1 Click on Map with internet connection to enjoy the interactive map

New Zealand Public Holidays 2018

Keeping in mind that New Zealanders love to take their holidays during summer, the busiest time is usually over the Christmas/ New Year period for about 4 weeks. If you don't like crowds and want to be able to pay more reasonable rates, my suggestion is to travel at a different time.

January: New Year's celebration: January 1st and 2nd

February: Waitangi Day, February 6th

March: Good Friday: March 30th

April: Easter Monday: April 2nd, ANZAC Day: April 25th

May: No Public holidays

June: Queens Birthday weekend 4th of June

July: No Public holidays

August: No Public holidays

September: No Public holidays

October: Labor Day: 22nd of October

November: No public holidays

December: Christmas Day: 25th of December, Boxing Day 26th of December.

Printed in Great Britain
by Amazon